FREE
"Overcoming addiction through the power of God."

Memory Bengesa

©2017, 2018 by Memory Bengesa
First published by Verengai Publishing House
1/20/2018

ISBN-978-0-9995371-1-4

FREE Overcoming addiction through the power of God
Copyright © 2012 by Memory Bengesa. All rights reserved. Printed in the United States of America. No part of this book may be used or reproduced in any manner whatsoever without the written consent of its author.
www.MemoryBengesa.com

"So, if the Son sets you free, you will be free indeed."
—John 8:36

CONTENTS

Dedication 6
Introduction 7
CHAPTER 1 10
How did I get here? 10
CHAPTER 2 13
How was the seed sown? 13
CHAPTER 3 20
What is going on with me? 20
CHAPTER 4 27
Why Me? 27
CHAPTER 5 30
A Glimpse of Hope 30
PURSUIT OF SOBRIETY 39
CHAPTER 6 42
Rejoice in H.O.P.E 42
CHAPTER 7 44
Be Patient in Tribulation 44
CHAPTER 8 46
Be Constant in Prayer 46
CHAPTER 9 48
The Claws of the Devourer 48
S.I.N 51
CHAPTER 10 55
Lured 55
CHAPTER 11 58
Enticed 58
CHAPTER 12 61
Desire 61
DELIVERED 63
CHAPTER 13 64

Faith 64
CHAPTER 14 66
Believe 66
CHAPTER 15 69
Know 69
FREE 70
CHAPTER 16 72
The Principal Ingredient 72
CHAPTER 17 74
Redemption 74
CHAPTER 18 78
Reconciliation 78
CHAPTER 19 80
Restored 80

Dedication

This book is dedicated to that person whose fleshly desire supersedes spiritual desire, so much so that they are now held hostage by it. I write from my experience of a nine-year bondage to substance and nicotine, and how today, I am living absolutely free; free from cravings and the confines of addiction.

Introduction

What typically comes to mind when certain people hear the word "addiction" is substance abuse, as majority quickly but wrongly subsume all concepts of addiction under that one component. An "addiction" can, however, be manifested in all areas of a person's life. Addiction is simply a lack of control over desires of one's flesh, of which substance abuse is a part. While this book is primarily based on the experiences of a one-time substance addict, it also lays a great informational foundation for all other types of addiction struggles. Its sole purpose is to shed spiritual light on the warfare of bondage, rather than to attempt to highlight the "demerits" of one form of addiction over another.

Our world tends to classify addiction according to the perceived severity of individual circumstances, but this book attempts to level all addictions into one single plain, in order to effectively empower Christians in the struggle against the flesh. So, whether it is alcohol, drugs, pornography, food, non-alcoholic beverages, money, power, materialism; whatever it is that has caused your flesh to consistently manipulate you, you can find help herein. A Christian should always be led by the Spirit, but once the enemy finds an enabling distraction in your life, he creates a deceptive temporary escape in the form of addiction.

This habit tends to pleasure you so much that no matter how hard you try, your flesh refuses to let go. You must, however, understand that continuos subordination to the leadings of the flesh will result in bondage to sin, which ultimately can lead to death. But cheer up! You are the reason I have been sent. My prayer for you is that by the time you have completed this book, you will be loosed from the struggles that have held you back from being God's profitable servant, in the name of Jesus.

I am not proud of my past; matter of fact, I hate the sin I have exposed myself to. However, it's a part of my life I never dwell on, as I press forward for the prize of the high calling in Jesus Christ. I would have preferred not to relive these experiences, but necessity has been laid on me. I made God a promise as I went the through dark days and long years of seeking healing, "If you heal me of my addiction, I will help all that suffer from addiction." I was not so concerned about "how" I would help ALL addicts, neither did I envision it in the form of a book at the time. Earlier this year, God reminded me of that promise and went on to honor my sincere desire in the most unprecedented way; the gift of writing went aglow in my spirit. I can't help but think He must have had this planned out all along.

This book does not intend to impress you with an excellent scholarly point of view on addiction, rather, it exposes a real person's journey through the physical and mental anguish of addiction for nine years. I am however incredibly excited that the past is indeed gone forever, and I am so proud that I found Jesus, the only begotten Son of God whom the Father sent to die for all our sins so that today, I can enjoy this "abundant life" that gave me absolute freedom from addiction. Addiction is at an all-time high in our nation and the world. Many families are being torn apart by its evil entity, while others come face to face with death at its tenacious hands. Rehabilitation centers cost a little less than a fortune, and the uninsured are going without help while the insured are getting the help they need, some of whom may relapse in some cases, for the worse. The bottom line is, we have a silent pandemic on our hands. I have been through rehabilitation, support meetings, and relapses yet nothing worked for me except the BLOOD of Jesus. Sheer will was never strong enough.

Please understand that by my prior statement, I do not seek to discourage you from whatever course you are currently charting towards maintaining sobriety. I only wish to use this book as proof of God's healing power. I am calling on the name of Jesus, pleading the blood of Jesus and depending on the Holy Spirit to tear down every addiction bondage and stronghold in your life. And through the reading of this book, your healing will flow unhindered to you as it did me.

Beloved, I love and thoroughly enjoy this new life, and I sincerely want the same for you. I am excited about what God has in store for me both now and in the future. I have so much compassion for addicts because I was one so I know how difficult it is to be unable to let go, and how embarrassing circumstances can emanate from addiction; the shame, guilt, running in with the law and the feelings of helplessness and hopelessness that come with it. I spent too many years at the mercy of the enemy and almost lost my life twice. But I have also come to know the healing faucet…it is free, sure and available to all. It is the BLOOD of Jesus. I sincerely hope that you will come to understand the deliverance inherent in the blood of Jesus and the great promises that God has for us all.

For I know the plans I have for you, declares the LORD, plans for welfare and not for evil, to give you a future and hope.
–Jeremiah 29:11

CHAPTER 1

How did I get here?
"The 'why' or 'how' answered helps the 'where' anticipated."—Memory Bengesa

One interesting pre-conceived notion held by most people is that addicts look a certain way, and thanks to "Hollywood," some people believe that stereotype. For instance, whenever we hear about a crack or cocaine addict, we automatically lean to the fact that they must be skinny and malnourished. We couldn't be more wrong, as every addict has their unique appearance, and it is not necessarily as dramatic or as frightening as we might have assumed. At the time of my bondage, I was what could be described as a functional addict. In other words, I was a regular, punctual, responsible person at work but once home after work hours, my addiction took over. Whether you're an addict or you are considering helping one, be aware that they come in all forms and colors, not just in a particular stereotype.

I was raised in an average upper-middle-class suburban household in Zimbabwe, and my parents provided for us as best as they could. My family found Jesus, while I was in my early teenage years but it was still a new concept for me. Therefore, I could not grasp much of it beyond the childhood experience. My parents gave us a great life; exotic vacations in other countries, shopping, and extra-curricular sporting activities. At some point, I must have been playing three sports in different seasons, within the space of two years. Between elementary school and high school, I had managed to engage myself in tennis, field hockey, netball, basketball, relay, long-jump, short-jump, hurdles, discus, and very competitive swimming events. My teenage years were filled with eventful weekends marked by slumber parties, crazy boy-talk, and random movie theater hangouts. My parents had become fully active in the church but I only tagged along for their sake as the whole concept was largely unfamiliar to me. I had accepted Christ as my Lord and Savior at the age of twelve, but by the time I was getting into high school, my relationship with God had dwindled and my new high school friends were way "cooler" than God, or so I thought at the time.

I remember feeling "super-grown" in high school; I was not that scrawny-looking junior high girl anymore. It seemed that over the break just before high school, some "feminine goddess" had touched me in my sleep and my body had metamorphosed into the shapely form of a young lady, even though I was only thirteen. I had the type of curvy figure that some seniors could only dream of. I was young, naïve and unaware of the power of my developed body. My group of friends certainly did not help much, as we all looked older than our ages and seemed to constantly invite trouble. My biggest battle in high school was fighting off vicious rumors and haters; what we used to call "jealous girls."

My friends and I grew quite close and became almost inseparable. Blinded by the illusion of our grown bodies, we often hung around older kids, further deluding us into thinking we were invincible. In a nutshell, my high school journey was a shallow stage play of ignorance, where the single most important goal was maintaining a popularity code set in place by my clique of friends. Earlier in high school, we had faced some occasional minor reprimands from the Principal's office due to our reputation for mischief, but none of us had ever tried drugs or alcohol.

Now far away from the familiar milieu of Zimbabwe, my latter days in high school saw me calmer as I was now in America and had no friends. I was just acclimatizing to this new environment and culture, which somehow tamed me, and in the process, got me more focused in school. Although I had a job, my schoolwork remained my primary focus. I made a few great friends, but I largely kept to myself and my family as I was different. I was no longer the popular kid but rather the weird kid with the funny accent and the communication barrier seemed pretty wide. Unbeknownst to me, some more people had suddenly taken a great liking to me because I had managed to save my little paychecks and had bought a car. I quickly became the people's favorite especially on Friday and Saturday nights when someone was having a "house party." I eventually understood why my number of friends had increased and used it to my advantage as well; they became my ticket to numerous "garage parties" and gigs in the latter years of high school.

      What was interesting was that I sailed through all of those without ever experimenting with alcohol or drugs. Drugs never caught my fancy, especially because my mother had vehemently warned us against having any such hard drug ties, before arriving the United States. Her warning had played on my naivete, so she managed to scare me off even the thought of experimenting with them. Of course, I was at parties and events where people engaged in such activities, but they never really caught my attention. For instance, I could never understand why people drank anything as bitter as alcohol. Yes, that was how I felt at the time, and I only knew it tasted that nasty because a friend offered me a sip at a party which I accepted, just to satisfy my curiosity as to what the hype was all about. I certainly wasn't impressed, neither could I get over how it reeked! Had anyone told me at that time that I would ever get dependent on alcohol, I would have laughed hard in their face and called them crazy.

CHAPTER 2

How was the seed sown?

"Addiction can be summarized as a false comfort that is usually brought about through one's trying times and the lack of knowledge and absence of God in dealing with the reality."
—Memory Bengesa

I graduated from high school earlier than my class. I met a guy through my friends, and we started dating not long after. My part-time job eventually became full-time as soon as I graduated. My life was fabulous; I had an early step into college, a fulltime job at a restaurant, and a new boyfriend who loved me. For the purpose of this book, I'll call him "Tony." The first six to eight months of our relationship went quite well but while I went to work and took part-time college classes, Tony, however, had no desire for work. Whenever I reflect on why I even spent time with him, I realize it must have been out of a need for a meaningful relationship, somehow feeling that he would be the ideal boyfriend for a committed relationship. Looking back, there certainly were awkward moments which could have helped me discern that he was all wrong for me, had I walked in the Spirit. I suppose I was too "giddy" to realize it was a superficial love relationship.

Tony was apparently struggling with some form of substance dependence, and by the time I found out, I had become too blinded by my intense feelings for him, to stop seeing him. Although I never found his habit impressive nor enticing, sooner than later, our lives become increasingly intertwined. Tony and I started spending more and more time with each other to the point that he would attend college classes with me. On Christmas Eve that same year, I got off work late. Tony had begged me to see him that evening before going home, so I reluctantly stopped over at his place. Though unemployed, he had an apartment, and his mom was paying his rent. I arrived at his place, and we exchanged gifts to celebrate Christmas Eve. With a case of beer, he indulged himself in his habit and then offered me a bottle. I stared at him, wide-eyed. I expected him to have known better as I wasn't given to alcohol and drugs. He laughed hysterically, half-mocking my refusal to drink. I ignored his goading remarks and stood my ground while he kept pressing. I had tried a sip a while back and threw it out, so I knew it was gross, but Tony insisted that maybe I wasn't drinking it quite right as if I would have known there was a right or wrong way to it. We went back and forth until I eventually caved in and said, "Fine! I will drink just half, not the whole bottle." Tony was so surprised I had finally agreed, that before I could change my mind, he hurriedly grabbed a bottle from the refrigerator and walked towards me while trying to open it.

    He handed me the open bottle of beer while clutching his and gave me a "tutorial" on how to "effectively" drink the nasty stuff. He asked me to watch closely as he demonstrated, however, I found nothing different from the usual method of drinking water, in the way he drank his. I was a little confused and reluctant. He gave me the go-ahead, but I hesitantly placed the bottle underneath my nose to smell first. I frowned at how horrible it smelled.

    He laughed and told me to pinch my nose, tilt my head back and "chug" the whole bottle; I surely thought he had lost his mind. I placed the bottle down on the coffee table and continued to watch TV. I had never been one to cave so easily beneath peer pressure, but for some reason, his words of instigation began to poke at me, and my immature mind suddenly raged to prove him wrong. In that moment, all I remember is that I picked up the bottle of now semi-cold beer, held my nose shut, tilted my head back and "chugged" the whole twelve-ounce bottle of bitterness, with some of it running out of the corners of my mouth, yet I refused to stop till I was done. After downing the whole bottle, I slammed it on the table and felt an awkward sensation in my stomach. I thought I was going to puke so I grabbed my stomach with one hand and held my mouth shut with the other; something was definitely rising through my throat. What I thought would be vomit, turned out to be one big burp; the loudest burp I'd ever done in my life! I was embarrassed, but now, I was feeling somewhat loose in the legs and arms and could not help but laugh, and so did Tony. Despite the tingling feeling in my legs and hands, I had to go to the restroom, and it was not until I tried to stand up that I realized the intensity of that little twelve-ounce bottle. When I got up, it felt like all the blood rushed to my head and the room was in slow motion. I remember thinking to myself, "What is this feeling? I like it." I managed to get to the bathroom, and by the time I returned and sat down to watch TV, it appeared I had found my new "happy place."

That strange sensation felt so relaxing; Tony was talking to me, but I couldn't properly connect with the conversation through the haze. I was "buzzing." That night, I had tasted something that was nasty on the tongue but exhilarating to the senses. Every time I hung around Tony after that, he made sure he had a drink for me. Looking back, I think he just sought to hook me onto something while he nursed his addiction, but I did not realize at the time, as I was still reveling in the false ecstasy the drinks were providing.

As our relationship grew longer, it also became increasingly damaging as I fully discovered Tony's true colors. Each time we hung out together, it seemed to always result in horrendous arguments that left me raiding his refrigerator, one drink after the other. It seemed that as the arguments multiplied, so did my desperation for a release through having more drinks. His possessive nature had unmasked itself into dangerous jealousy, which then became insecurity and snowballed into violence. At that point in such a toxic relationship, I was drinking a twenty-four-ounce can of beer (tall boy) a night. Alcohol had become the fuel that was supposedly getting me through a meaningless relationship. Please understand that I am not blaming my addiction on my failed relationship. However, the horrible circumstances aided my growing desire to drink. My relationship kept plummeting till I could no longer stand it.

Tony kept getting worse and so was I with the alcohol. I had begun to fear for my life and that of my family as he had also made a habit of threatening myself and my family whenever I attempted to end the relationship. I was well aware of his anger management problems as well as his strong ties with a notorious southern Californian gang so, I was terrified of his violent tendencies. I figured the only way to exit the relationship safely was to hatch a deceptive plot. I lied that I had decided to relocate to the Mid-West (Kansas), as my best friend had just moved there.

The plan took months to set in motion before I could eventually present it as an airtight story to Tony. I, however, refrained from telling him the exact day I would be leaving town. When the day came, my best friend, along with another friend, flew one way to California, from where we then took a road trip to Kansas. I planned to stay there for the three months of summer and return in time for the fall semester, in hopes of picking up my life where I left off, without Tony of course. Upon arriving to Kansas, my best friend got me a little summer job that kept me mostly occupied, but whenever I was off, I recklessly indulged in my new addiction. Tony was now hundreds of miles away, and I was no longer afraid for my life, yet I continued to drink every night as if my body depended on it. I had become a "functioning alcoholic," and I didn't even know it! I was quite young and had casually thought that it was just one of those things young college people got up to. My friends did not think much of it either, as they too would join me for a drink now and then, especially since we literally partied all summer.

My drinking worsened as I continued to bottle up the details of my abusive relationship. My friends had no idea why I left Califonia that summer; all they knew was that I had just purchased a spanking new car and I convinced them that we needed a road trip in it. That seemed to satisfy them, so they got on board. I was hurting deeply because I genuinely cared for this "street-thug" boyfriend but could not get myself to open up about it to anyone. Drinking seemed to momentarily numb my heartache, so it only made sense for me to continue the habit in order to sustainably repress my pain and drown my thoughts. I was always angry, often hurling rude, sharp words at anyone who crossed me even in the slightest way.

I was terribly hurting and transferred aggression on others. My alcohol tolerance levels had increased so much that there was now only one way to end my evenings; reveling in drinks in such a way that I did not need to dwell too much on the events of the day. Moving to the Midwest for that summer gave me some peace and security, but it did not make my drinking situation any better because I was emotionally scarred from the verbal and mental abuse. At this time in my life, I still did not think I had a problem, after all, this was what other college kids did.

"Your circumstances are not the engine of addiction rather; a justification of those circumstances becomes the pilot of acceptance for addiction." —Memory Bengesa

The weeks flew by, fall arrived, and the time finally came for me to return to the west coast. I literally snuck back into the state of California under the radar to prevent Tony from finding out about my return as he was now probably convinced that I was gone for good. Upon arrival, I carried on with my life with no inclination of the drinking habit that kept consuming me. The hardest thing for me years later was admitting that I had a problem. As I reflect on those years, I realize that I placed myself in the worst of situations because I allowed my flesh to hold me bound to alcohol, and that created an opening for other negative feelings to latch on, such as insecurity. My insecurities led me into more meaningless relationships, often promoting my habit. I was always angry and insensitive; a volcano waiting to erupt. Once settled into life in California, I got right back on the social scene and reconnected with all my friends, except Tony of course.

It's almost unbelievable how I pulled off so much all at once, but I can certainly say God's hand was on me, even then. I traveled with a car full of change of clothes, books, and work uniforms; no matter what, I could do any of the three, but regardless of which I did, every night was a night to party. I partied Monday through Monday; from Los Angeles to Beverly Hills to Las Vegas to Palm Springs, there was no slowing down in my circle of friends. About three years after returning to California, I graduated from college. My first job afforded me the opportunity to travel around the country. In pursuit of full-time employment, I landed a position with a privately-owned company that returned me to the Mid-West, though not Kansas this time.

With each new experience of moving to a city in which I knew no one, my alcohol consumption kept escalating, except this time, it was all me, with no friends to blame it on. At this point, I must have begun to use alcohol to mask my loneliness. I had no relationship with Christ, having departed from Christ at the age of thirteen, chasing the lies of the world. By now, I was consuming one six-pack case of alcoholic beverage per night.

I only vaguely remember my nights, as I would usually get off work, stop by the local convenience store to purchase my six-pack, go on to a neighboring restaurant to purchase food, and thereafter head home to my quaint apartment and shut myself in. I would get out of my work clothes and into my pajamas, then go right back to the living room, where my food sat on the coffee table right next to my carton of beer. I did not bother to place my beer in the refrigerator, as I wanted to just get right into my ritual. I would find my favorite shows on cable and launch into my drinking spree, one bottle after another till all six were gone. By then, it would be the wee hours of the night, and I would open my box of food and start to eat mindlessly till it was gone.

My ultimate satisfaction arose from the complex combination of a full stomach and a tipsy mind. After dozing off and passing the night on the couch, I would wake early the following morning, take a shower, get dressed and leave for work, grabbing along a gallon of water to keep me hydrated throughout the day. When that work day was over, I would repeat the same cycle. I had no clue that the most enslaving part of my addiction was really in my perpetual disinterest in anything else after work, other than to drink, eat and sleep, even on the weekends. This cycle continued for some years.

> *"Bondage is the leading gateway to all other sinful manifestations in your life."* —Memory Bengesa

CHAPTER 3

What is going on with me?

"The escalation of bondage can leave you feeling as if your flesh is being held hostage."
—Memory Bengesa

It was one of those Saturdays that I was home, running through my predictable routine; I woke up, cleaned my apartment, ran a few errands, paid bills, stopped at the store for groceries and alcohol, and then headed back home in the afternoon. I had made a habit of buying tons of alcohol during the weekends so I would not have to leave my apartment for more, and because I was not going to work, I felt I could drink more than usual and have my binge of TV time. That afternoon, as I sat down to watch my favorite network, I remember watching a documentary about addiction called "Intervention." Of course, at this time, I still did not think I was an addict, but the documentary had left me somewhat intrigued. I started contemplating purchasing a home during that period, and for the first time in the seven years of drinking, I felt that maybe, just maybe, I needed to at least "check" if I was over-consuming alcohol. I, however, did not feel any urgency to perform this check in my alcohol use.

I continued with my drinking routine. I remember that one of the few concerns that started to crop up was my health. By now, I was at my heaviest (250 pounds) as I did not practice any healthy eating habits. I began to realize the damage to which I was subjecting my body, but was still unable to quit because, in my mind, I did not have an alcohol problem. It had occurred to me a few times that maybe I was drinking a bit too much, but it never really dawned on me that I was an alcoholic. Now that I have become sober, that way of thinking certainly feels weird. And this is also the bewildered question of the non-addict; they think "Why don't you just put it down?!" As much as that makes sense, I am here to testify that it was a fight for my life. My body had become accustomed to the alcohol, and I wanted more and more each day. Though I would try to stop, I could not. In my spiritual opinion, I could not "just stop drinking." I was bound to an entity that would not let me quit. Being a Spirit-filled, born-again believer, I now know that I was *bound* back then.

It was never about having the jitters or shakes when I did not drink; it was just that I always felt like I simply had to drink. The thought of getting a drink weighed heavily on my mind throughout the day, and when I was getting ready to get off work, it was the same thought on my mind. In fact, I would get super-excited towards just thinking about it. My flesh was in constraints to this evil entity, but at this time, I did not know that, neither had it registered in my mind that I was bound, since I was not a Christian yet. One day, while drinking the night away on my couch, I eventually got to a point where I felt like I had drank all that I could possibly drink. For the first time, somewhere in my heart, I chose to acknowledge that there was a problem with the amount of alcohol I was consuming. In spite of this priceless moment of sanity, I still had not accepted that I was an addict.

How could I be? "Addicts" were supposedly junkies; unemployed people who got drunk and high all day, with no goals in life. That certainly wasn't me. I worked a job, always arrived there on time, and never called in sick. I might have had a hangover, but water and pills took care of that. I was always well groomed with hair and nails perfectly in place so, in my opinion, I could not be an addict; I just drank too much and finally felt that I needed help in cutting back on what I drank.

I entertained the idea of rehabilitation in my head for the next couple of weeks. I finally decided to begin the search for nearby rehabilitation centers, on the internet. I had dragged it out in my mind for so long because I felt I simply did not have the time to go for an In-patient program. I had a job and couldn't see it working so I never bothered until this particular night when I eventually contacted some professionals. Of course, I did not comprehend the procedures of rehabilitation centers. My call that night proceeded almost as if what I wanted was a confirmation that my drinking was fine and that way, I could mentally try to fix it all on my own because really, no one wants to be labeled an "addict."

As I continued my research, the enemy kept throwing overwhelming questions of "what if's" my way. I remember one of them being, "What if I am an addict, I do not have time to do all the meetings…" My mind was racing, but I knew this had to be done as I had started feeling as if I was slowly dying on the inside. I finally found an outpatient center and went through the initial screening process to assess if I was an addict. I remember the lady on the phone placing me on hold and getting a counselor, and then I remember the counselor going through the same series of questions already asked by the first lady.

The questions were pretty straightforward, and by the time I was done responding, it was obvious that my alcohol consumption per day qualified me as an alcoholic. She urged me to come in as soon as possible to begin my recovery clinics. And because she could not believe how much alcohol I was consuming per day, she was quite concerned about the side effect of going "cold turkey." Her words of advice to me were, "Please, consult with your family physician before starting our program so they can give you medication for the side effects, because a person that consumed as much alcohol as I did daily for all those years could risk going into cardiac arrest due to shock if I chose to go cold turkey without medication from a doctor. "This could be death in disguise."

"Wow!" I thought, completely freaked out by her words, as the idea of death did not sit well with me. Unbeknownst to me, I had been consuming a tremendously dangerous amount of alcohol over the years. After speaking with the counselor, I reasoned that I was not ready for rehab if the side effects might be worse than what I was already experiencing or if they could lead to death. You see, the enemy will try to talk you out of your attempts at recovery by every means possible. After some weeks of consideration, and watching my alcohol tolerance levels begin to rise again, I had to consult my physician, who was reluctant to give me a prescription medication to help me cope with my sobriety, for fear that I might slip into co-dependence.

I did not pursue it any further as I dreaded the possibility of getting hooked on pills, so I decided to go "cold turkey" upon beginning treatment. Never in my wildest dreams could I have imagined myself in rehab, yet there I was, finally in the "circle"; the circle I had despised all those years. I called it the circle of shame and defeat! It made me feel like I had indeed been defeated by my addiction. I remember my first circle introduction, "Hello! My name is… Memory and I am an alcoholic. I have been sober for X and Y days." Everyone gave me a warm welcome and clapped, applauding my sobriety. It was a difficult pill to swallow. All I could think was, *what went wrong?* How could this bright upper-middle class, metropolitan girl, raised by both parents, be an addict? Where did I go wrong? I had more questions than I could find answers.

"Bondage is not prejudice; it knows no boundaries, and exists only to demoralize its captives, causing God's people to fall."—Memory Bengesa

The hardest days were the first few days of rehab; here I was, trying to unravel a seven-year-old habit in a couple of days. This was something I had gotten so dangerously familiar with to the point that, it was all I had done every single night after work. Although it was exciting to be able to see the world through sober lenses for the first time in a long time, and I was gradually becoming more hopeful as days turned into weeks, I still wasn't quite sure what to make of it all. I was in the process of learning to control the amount of alcohol I drank, but I still had yet to fully come to terms with actually being an "addict." I could not wrap my now sober mind around the fact that I would never have another drink, ever in my life; not on my birthday, not on Christmas Eve, not on New Year's Eve, not on the 4th of July—never! Man! That was the hardest truth I had to deal with. Sure, rehab encouraged us to live a day at a time, but my thoughts kept getting ahead of me. My greatest challenges in my quest to attain sobriety seemed to stem primarily from the direction of my thoughts.

Despite these unsteady thoughts, I was doing well in my outpatient care, and was able to keep the entire process from everyone else; no one knew, not even my family or my closest friends. I simply did not have time to explain and besides, I was embarrassed by the fact that I was in rehab.

This shame also sprang out of my faulty perspective of who an addict really was. I felt that if I ever told anyone, they would judge me just as harshly as I had judged addicts. I resolutely remained in outpatient care, and upon the completion of my recovery program, I felt a sense of accomplishment, as though I was ready to take on the world. I was super-psyched that I had managed to be sober for eight full weeks. I was given a book containing the schedule with all the group meetings in my area, and with a firm resolve to defeat the addiction, I attended some meetings and managed to maintain sobriety. Never forget that the enemy doesn't give up easily and will attempt to steer you off the right course. One of the first few events I attended after my program was a baseball game and it was my first game ever. My co-worker had tickets with great seats.

Now here is the absolute kicker; her retired father was the "beer-guy" at the stadium. I initially did not think that was going to be a problem. I was in fact, feeling quite resilient on this particular day, as the beer in the stadium was selling at what could only be regarded as "daylight robbery" prices, and I was certain that I wasn't in the least bit willing to spend that kind of money. That served as an excellent mental deterrent until I saw my co-worker's dad continually making trips around us, offering us some beer! Yes! For free! I was a bit shaken but needless to say; I passed that first test. Months after rehab, reality started setting in.

I knew I did not want to spend the rest of my life attending somber meetings… so, I stopped going; apparently my first mistake. Now if you're reading this, and meetings do work for you, please keep attending. This is merely an expression of my experience. For me, the most dreaded part of meetings was that I constantly found myself driving all over town to find one; another sacrifice for sobriety that is actually well worth it.

The people at the meetings were great, but I was also convinced that this was a part of my life that I wanted to end completely without having to remember it ever again. Someday soon I hoped to get married and have a family, and I certainly would not like to have to scurry off to a meeting, smack-dead in the middle of my family dinner for instance. I wanted to travel the world, without any burdensome thoughts of needing to find a rehab meeting in every new city and or country. I wanted to live a sober life; one that was free of any reminders of my drinking days.

With all these nagging thoughts tumbling through my mind, I eventually gave up on the meetings prematurely, without even giving them a chance. Indeed, the greatest battleground for my addiction was my mind. Little wonder that it is also always the devil's first target. No sooner had I stopped attending meetings I found myself back at square one; relapse. My property construction was already ongoing at this time, and it had made for excellent motivation for my alcohol discipline.

I felt like I had to manage my finances properly in order to adequately fund my relocation and was also looking forward to the positive impact of a new environment on my blooming sobriety. Alcohol had been the major driver of my emotions and feelings for so many years such that I was more or less disconnected from sober reasoning. I was in the middle of a lot and encountered a heart-wrenching moment, and simply because I wasn't yet skilled at handling my emotions soberly, I went running back to the bar.

That first drink, after months of abstinence, felt like I had never even quit. I should have known better about triggers had I continued with my meetings and gotten a sponsor; someone that could have helped me stay the sober course. After the first few drinks, I felt nothing at all, and that encouraged me to keep going until I finally felt that strange yet familiar effect course through my body; my drinking tolerance had yet increased. The devil tried to play mind games with me, and my weak defense was to take refuge in denial. I did not want to feel as though I had been defeated with the relapse, so I thought if I could ration how much I drank this time, then I did not really have a problem. I was trying to act like I had self-discipline because surely, if I could control my alcohol intake, then that meant that I was normal like any other social drinker, right? Well, I was wrong.

While I was drinking less in terms of volume, I was actually drinking more based on alcohol percentage. I used to drink a six-pack of beer before rehab, so this time, after my relapse, I would buy two tall cans of beer, which were 24 ounces each, and then I would buy a 24-ounce bottle of a sparkling flavored alcoholic beverage that I would mix with a pocket-size bottle of vodka. For me, it all came down to the metrics and anyway, that's what addicts do; find a way to keep getting drunk or high. So, though it seemed to my alcoholic's mind that it wasn't a six-pack, it was still undoubtedly more alcohol.

This was the beginning of the darkest days of my life. My addiction level before rehab was certainly "child's play" compared to my experiences in relapse. I began to feel as though my flesh would heat up when it was time to drink. I still wasn't having tremors when I didn't drink, but I was definitely tense as work hours came to a close each day. The bondage was stronger and tougher; it was out for blood, it was out to lead me to utter body rot, and ultimately, death. At this point in my life, I had to have a drink after work; there were no ifs or maybes.

> *"The devil wants to destroy the modern-day temple (your body) in mockery of God through the bondage of addiction."*
> *—Memory Bengesa*

CHAPTER 4

Why Me?

"Justification can be the catalyst of evil thought manifestation." — Memory Bengesa

What should have been the happiest times of my life, became my darkest seasons. After my relapse, my addiction returned with a vehement vengeance. There was no stopping myself from drinking; in fact, it felt as though I had never attended rehab. I just could not understand all that was happening to me. I was now living in my full-fledged addiction, yet constantly seeking to deny that I was an addict. I resignedly succumbed to the "if you can't beat them, join them," mentality and got so tired of fighting my addiction that I just gave into its dark clutches, drinking without inhibition. All through that period, I had moments in which I wondered when I was going to stop abusing alcohol. I was not necessarily asking God that question; I just wondered.

Every time I came close to quitting, I seemed to quickly enlist the help of a familiar friend; he is called "justification." I would find myself somehow rationalizing the need for my habit. This false self-justification made me feel better at that moment when in truth, I simply was suffering from a bad habit. I now realize that *justifications are the green cards our mind provides in order to rationalize our actions and give us a license to do the wrong thing.* I have come to understand fully, through God's wisdom, the negative power of justification. The more you justify yourself in a bad habit, the wider the gates of your mind open to admit evil and negative thoughts to manifest and eventually come alive into actions. Understand that when you justify wrong actions, its equivalent to calling an evil thing good, thus making an excuse to do whatever it is that you want, and excuses are the gateways to strongholds. Those who are bound to an evil lifestyle, certainly do not initially volunteer for bondage. It just usually begins with a small, seemingly harmless step, which then progresses through a path filled with various "good" excuses and self-justifying actions, eventually giving way to a stronghold.

Have you ever paid attention to a person that justifies themselves? You would be sadly fascinated by their thought pattern. I once knew a person in his thirties who told me that he had been smoking marijuana since the age of 15. He went on to say that marijuana does not have the same effect on him as it does to everyone else and that he keeps smoking because it helps him focus on the job and deal with the people at work.

His boss probably never even realized he was always under the influence. This individual is a great example; here is someone that has already made up a deeply ingrained excuse to smoke marijuana, and it has become so real to him that he actually believes that daily use of the substance is for his benefit. His habit has thus become a stronghold, costing him the money he barely even has. Imagine the financial waste when you multiply the daily purchase by weeks and months and years. This was money he could have invested; little wonder that addicts live from paycheck to paycheck, struggling to keep feeding their stronghold.

I could not admit that I had a drinking problem because I did not want a life devoid of drinks as that would seem like a boring life. Drinking was all I had come to know, yet when I drank in excess, I hated it. In spite of this, I would justify my actions in a bid to deal with the fight between my flesh and spirit. My little excuses developed into long-term rationales that sucked out my cash long before pay-day because I was spending a lot of money each day, that certainly ran into tens of thousands of dollars a year!

> *"The enemy's way will always be the way of self-justification while God's way is always that of rational and Spirit-led discernment."* —Memory Bengesa

Of course, I can only make these calculations based on hindsight. While I was still in bondage, all that mattered was that I had enough money to keep my habit going. It was all about satisfying the gnawing desires of my flesh "right now," I had no foresight nor goals for the future. Bondage is designed to keep its captive tied to an element that sucks them dry at the moment, while inadvertently causing them long-term damage as well. Sin is always about an action within a brief moment, aimed at producing instant gratification. In my addict's mind, all that ultimately seemed to matter was getting my fix "right now."

That drink only placed me in a temporary phase of superficial happiness as it was substance-induced. It could never produce any deep or lasting satisfaction. When I relapsed, I convinced myself that my ability to restrict myself to certain drinks, especially the one in just a tiny little bottle along with merely 2 "tall boys," meant I was at least in control of my drinking.

The truth, however, was that the combination of those got me the "buzz" I needed and was actually stronger than what I used to drink before then. My denial got so bad that I even presented a façade of sobriety to my friends. Whenever we got together, I would tell them that I was no longer drinking, yet I would carry an unsuspicious container with alcohol in it. I felt that successfully fooling other people somehow meant that maybe, I was indeed fine, or at least not as bad as it looked.

> *"A stronghold can only be broken when you stare it in the face and call it by its name and plead the blood of Jesus. As long as you remain in self-justification, you may never get free."*
> —Memory Bengesa

CHAPTER 5

A Glimpse of Hope

"In the midst of it all, God is still in control."
—Memory Bengesa

On this particular Saturday, it was summer time, I was home and had started drinking early, then soon dozed off on the couch. When I woke up, I felt a need to go out. I wanted to get in my car and just go somewhere, but I kept fighting the feeling as I was comfortable on my couch. I kept feeling the nudge to go in the car and drive out, so eventually, I got off my couch and decided to go. I got all dolled up and grabbed my purse, opting to go and take a walk on the strip of an area that was known for great weekend entertainment. I arrived on this strip and parked in great spot.

I glanced up in the direction of what looked like a quaint bar, "maybe I could get a drink there," I thought. As I was heading towards the bar, three gentlemen were walking towards me on the strip, and my eyes locked with one of them. I smiled and kept walking, then one of the guys from the group approached me. Thoughts of the little bar just ahead distracted me while he introduced himself, but I couldn't help but notice how sweet and polite he was. Our conversation turned out to be quite interesting, and I enjoyed the unique experience of being ministered to on the streets. I was used to the usual boring pattern of eventually exchanging numbers, but this particular guy asked me what I was doing "tomorrow," a Sunday.

I got excited and told him I had no plans, then asked him what he had in mind. He said he would be going to church and invited me to go with him. Well! That was certainly a first; no guy had ever invited me to church. I felt like I was not ready, so I told him we could exchange numbers and I would get back to him on the "whole church" thing. I had not been in a church in years and did not even know where to start with his offer. I proceeded to the bar that evening but could not even finish my drink as thoughts of the earlier conversation wouldn't leave my mind.

I abandoned my drink and left for home. The following morning, I got a text from the same guy once again asking me to go with him to church, but I ignored it and stayed home. That Sunday afternoon, he called to check in on me and wanted to hang out in the park, so we met in the park and had such a fun and engaging conversation. He kept talking about church and how I lived close to his church and that I should check it out. At that time, I was too far gone into my selfish addiction to bother with a church trip, but he never gave up on me, and towards the end of the first week after we met, he invited me to church yet again. I finally agreed to attend, though I was a bit nervous.

He picked me up that Sunday morning, and we went together, arriving just a few minutes into the service. I remember being greeted by a warm, welcoming ambiance as we stepped in and took our seats. After the service, the pastor had a chat with me, and his powerful words touched my heart. "God has great plans for you," he said. I also met his beautiful wife who was ever so kind and sweet. My cute new friend drove me home, and from that day forward, my quest for God was ignited, as I started attending this church every Sunday. I still had an ongoing issue with my addiction. However, one thing I never stopped doing was going to church. The more I went to church, the closer I felt to being healed. It was so surreal that I could sense healing was real close by; I had gotten to a point in my life where I did not understand why I continued to drink. It was as if I only did it because I did not know another way to live. The most humiliating part of my addiction was running in with the law, having arguments with great friends, and broken relationships. Another sad thing about my addiction was this isolation as though I were a hermit; I did not want to be around anyone but myself and the alcohol. Those were the darkest days of my life. I started to hate drinking, but I would do it anyway. I hated stopping by the local convenience store because they already knew what I was going to get and worse still, they knew me on a first name basis. But I also believe that these were some of the series of events that led to my complete healing.

> *"You have to believe to receive."*—*Memory Bengesa*

    I had an interesting conversation with a great friend over lunch, and I was talking to her about my healing from addiction; she too had been struggling with a habit for a while. I mentioned to her that I knew I was healed because I never stopped believing that my healing was coming. On hearing that, my friend responded resignedly, saying she did not think she was ever going to stop. She said, "I guess you were hopeful," and that is exactly what we have to do in our quest for healing. You have to be hopeful and never give up on yourself. It didn't matter what stage I was; I knew that God was going to heal me eventually.

    We have to understand that this is a spiritual battle, complicated by the fact that there is no physical form before you to throw punches at, rather you are fighting the flesh, hidden in the guise of your own desires. The battle between flesh and spirit is always intense, and that's why the Bible is available to equip us for daily challenges. There were times it felt like the end was nowhere in sight yet I never gave up on God or conceded defeat.

    The fact that I was back in church did not mean that I received instant healing. In fact, the attacks on my flesh seemed to become magnified, and I still found myself repeatedly giving in to my fleshly desires. I understand now that the temptations heightened because the enemy was desperate to pull me out of church and out of the covering of God. The enemy knew that I was a step away from entering the realm of truth and completely being set free. I kept reminding myself that I was in my season and that healing was near. I kept thinking, "Don't give up on yourself Memory, not until you at least see what God has in store for you."

Right in the midst of my addiction, I would mentally envision myself looking healthy, and would even write a list of all the things I was hoping to do once I got healed.

You have to believe God to receive your healing; trust me, it works! God will heal you, and the blood of Jesus will restore you. You are not reading from an individual that happened to like to drink alcohol, but one who had gotten neck deep in chronic alcoholism. I can't count the number of times I relapsed and was constantly told that I was at death's door if I continued to drink at that rate. That is why I am so excited to bear testimony to the healing power in the blood of Jesus.

As you decide to involve yourself in church, be assured that you will be healed, but understand that healing is a process. Prepare to commit to that process. Our Father works in miraculous ways such that everything you will go through till you get completely healed will contain profound lessons with which He will build you up. Take hold of each moment as it comes and allow God to transform you from the inside out so that when healing comes, you are well equipped to flourish in it.

The first thing church did for me was to open my eyes to see my rot and my need. Only then did my struggle for life, and the need to save myself from irretrievable ruin, begin. This certainly was a spiritual battle; the moment I found God, the devil immediately felt threatened and further threw his weight in, to intensify the temptation. The issue was not my addiction in itself, but rather why I had that addiction. I depended on alcohol to numb and suppress my hurts from teenage years, into early adulthood. God started to work in me and convict me of these initial feelings I had tried to bury, and I became more and more sensitive to His transformation. I realized that when I returned to church, it was no longer about my addiction but about being as close to God as I could be. The more I went to church, the hungrier I was for God and as that hunger consumed me, so did his workings in me.

At one of our retreats, I received the Holy Spirit, and I knew then I was embarking on deeper spiritual warfare. After that, I was baptized in water, and I desired to live a holy life, but once again, I was still battling my addiction. As a result of this, I was really ashamed of myself as I felt that I was letting God down. Of course, now I realize that I was not exercising the full armor of God and I was not reading the Bible or fasting.

Although I was attending church and experiencing some growth, whenever I was at home, I reverted to my old ways. I was now a believer in Christ, so I recognized my sin for what it was, and it made falling into it repeatedly, all the more unbearable. Sometimes I got so desperate that I would begin to pray and cry in the midst of my binge drinking. Even when I felt defeated, I would actively denounce being called an alcoholic; I just knew that I would be healed. However, it was difficult to project when exactly that would happen while struggling through the journey. And that is why it is important to have hope.

H.O.P.E – Having an Optimistic Perspective on Everything

Believe to receive your healing. This comes through faith and trust in God and remaining hopeful that God has not forgotten about you. Members of the working class get up every day to go to work, knowing they would get paid at the designated time; that is great faith. Objectively speaking; however, job security really isn't guaranteed, because we can wake up one day and the company we work for is declaring bankruptcy or a disaster could have destroyed our work buildings over the night, yet we get up each day and go in faith. We simply believe we would get paid for the hours put into the job. Here is the point of this analogy; Give God the same, if not more faith and trust that He will heal you.

Keep going to church, keep yourself busy with ministry, and keep thanking Him in advance even if the stronghold is not yet broken. You have to believe that it will be done. One of the things that kept me motivated on my journey to healing was having a *dream book*. This was a simple notebook wherein I wrote everything I was going to do when I became sober; simple things like taking walks in the park and enjoying the fresh air. My addiction had me indoors and drinking all the time, so I never had days in which I woke up and spontaneously decided to take a walk in the park. I was simply too occupied with thoughts of what I would drink each evening. That was my priority. I have since learned, that prioritizing anything above God is idolatry; our first passion and love is supposed to be God alone.

> *"Addictions are not just substance-related; addiction is anything that takes priority above God especially when having it provides a 'temporary' pleasure fix like a drug would do to an addict."—Memory Bengesa*

     Addiction, from a spiritual point of view, is a state in which you are no longer able to control your flesh, as though your flesh were to be holding you hostage in your own body. Addiction comes with a wide variety of manifestations, such as substance, food, money, materialism, sex, pornography, and other seemingly normal things that we allow to take over our flesh to the point of idolatry. It is important to recognize the different forms of addiction because, in recent times, people tend to refer to anything that isn't substance abuse, as just a "habit" and maybe by true definition, it is. But if we're not careful, that habit will consume us and put us in a permanent state of bondage. Of course, as with substance abuse, the first step is admitting it. So instead of joining the world to casually refer to all non-substance abuse as "habits," look them in the eye and call them what they really are so that you can lose yourself from their grip.

     Understand that even the non-substance addictions can lead to a Christian's downfall. For example, if a person has a food addiction, then that means the temple of the Lord gets recklessly assailed with unhealthy meals, giving way to damaging and debilitating health conditions, which may result in long-term disease. People then begin to rebuke the devil when that individual gets hospitalized, whereas, the problem could have been cut off at the root before it became permanent. It is true that the devil often capitalizes on our addiction to cause us further damage, but we initiated the problem, not the devil.

The devil comes in to take advantage by preventing you from confronting the problem and becoming ultimately free, and this may occur in the form of relapses. I believe that you can engage in spiritual warfare, only after you have acknowledged your error and turned to God for forgiveness and healing; this is the blunt truth. This book is not only designed to help individuals with substance abuse problems but also to help those with non-substance addictions. There is an urgency for all to understand that our bodies are a temple designed for God to dwell in, and as long as we keep desecrating the body, we will lose our peace of mind.

If we seek satisfaction in 'things' that can potentially harm the body, then we are doing God a disservice. We must recognize that for a believer, overcoming addiction is more of a spiritual battle than it is a simple matter of refusing peer pressure or worldly influence. No one willingly goes searching for a stronghold. However, it does manifest once a bad habit is left unchecked. This is why it is so important for believers to continually purge the flesh. Fasting and praying are excellent ways of achieving this while also strengthening our spirit-man for the spiritual battle.

The pre-conceived notion that a particular addiction is worse than another is so wrong. To put it quite bluntly, an addiction is simply an addiction ensnaring no matter what form it takes. So, whether it is coffee or alcohol, they share a common attribute; they exert control over their users. Alcoholism has adverse long-term consequences on the body, such as organ failure, while a caffeine addict may likely suffer headaches and jitters from withdrawals. These simply indicate that indeed, anything used in excess can create long-lasting fleshly hostage. One consequence may be worse than the other, but in the spiritual realm, the bottom line is the *flesh control*; allowing your flesh to be bound to anything that creates an entrance of weakness. *"A man without self-control is like a city broken into and left without walls"* *(Proverbs 25:28).*

"Addiction manifestation begins with the tongue, then takes root in the mind and becomes practical thereafter."
—*Memory Bengesa*

Proverbs 18:21 says *"Death and life are in the power of the tongue, and those who love it will eat its fruits,"* thus profoundly illustrating the incredible power of the words we speak. Be mindful of the statements you speak into your life, as those words eventually become real. Sometimes we say things we don't mean, not realizing that the devil latches on to such negativity and attempts to enact it in our lives. One summer, I got into the habit of having a bowl of my favorite ice cream, right before going to bed. It all began with a bowl here and there during the week. Then I started to say things like, *"I have to have a bowl of my favorite ice cream before I go to bed…otherwise, I would not be able to sleep."* I have underlined the two lies I affirmed in my mind, which eventually led me to the reckless habit of consuming ice cream every night, thus leading to weight gain.

As harmless as it initially appeared, I would have eventually become extremely obese had I continued with the habit. We have a family history of diabetes, so there is no telling which way the enemy would have taken me next. First and foremost, I did not "have" to have anything before I went to bed and secondly, I would be able to go to sleep; the ice cream did not put me to sleep. It only just made me feel good …and passive to the manifestation at hand. The statements we often use to describe those desires can trigger occurrences that eventually lead to bondage.

These days, when I sense an ungodly habit beginning to consume me, I back off "cold-turkey," sometimes with a jump-start of a fast, because I know that God will help me. Some people make statements like, *"That's my favorite drink; I have to have it so I can feel good,"* or *" I have to smoke a cigarette during every break… just to work with these people because they work my nerves so bad,"* or *"I have to get high before I go to work so I can have a productive day,"* or *"This video does contain full-on pornography…I am just watching it for entertainment purposes,"* or *" I cannot eat without a glass of wine,"* or *" I always have to have a king-size candy bar before I go to bed,"* and the list goes on.

You do not "have" to do anything. Do not justify yourself into bondage; self-justification only proves your incompetence at self-discipline. You are a believer, a child of God who doesn't have to do anything but love God and become bound to Christ. Fleshly justification can turn words into thoughts and thoughts into practical manifestation, resulting in a stronghold. Therefore, choose your words spiritually first, then wisely. Do not allow your flesh to rule you and seek spiritual discipline through fasting and praying too.

PURSUIT OF SOBRIETY

"Repent from your evil ways, turn away from your old self and be transformed in Christ Jesus and watch God become the only stronghold in your life."
—*Memory Bengesa*

I am glad that you made it this far in into this book, and I pray that the good Lord above grants you further understanding of salvation. Even as I write this book, I know that the devil is actively at his enterprise, but I have continually raised the power of the blood against him so that this body of work will indeed serve its purpose in effectively helping addicts recover. My greatest passion is that your spiritual eyes are flung open, and you obtain salvation and freedom through Christ.

It is no longer unfamiliar news that we are in warfare; one we do not see, and yet experience. Please understand that the problem is not the addict, but the addiction and the devil whose desire it is to keep his captive bound. I am often reminded of the weeds on a perfectly manicured lawn, growing out of rhythm and dampening the beauty of the field. The person with an addiction represents the lawn; beautiful in all their unique creation as a human being. The addiction then represents the weeds, growing out of line, diminishing that individual's great qualities and potential; the 'weeds' have obscured the good in him, much like a manicured lawn with dandelions in it. Well, one of the best-known methods of removing weeds is simply to pull them out at the roots!

This guarantees that nothing troublesome ever grows from that spot as the roots are no longer available to attach and re-grow. Likewise, the only way to be delivered from addiction is to attack the root of the problem, which is the enemy. He is the source of your addiction. Your battle is against the darkness of this world, eloquently sponsored by the devil and his army of demons; the outcasts of heaven, here on earth to terrorize mankind and to embody themselves in vessels (bodies) that are not Christ-filled! (Ephesians 6:10-20) The enemy never physically holds a gun to your head to cower you into an evil act. Instead, he works through your thoughts to engender the manifestation of strongholds.

If you want to be free, then get ready to take your stand, because when one is in pursuit of Sobriety through Christ, the enemy comes after you even harder. My countless attempts to regain a sober life seemed to further incite the enemy against me, making the battle fiercer and my relapses, numerous. In the next few chapters, I would like to share my thoughts on what to expect and what to do while in pursuit of sobriety.

> *"The Lord desires to dwell in us as long as we allow Him to but until then, one will walk around as an empty vessel that has a risk of being filled by evil entities."*
> — *Memory Bengesa*

CHAPTER 6

Rejoice in H.O.P.E

Rejoice in <u>hope</u>, be <u>patient</u> in <u>tribulation</u>, be <u>constant</u> in <u>prayer</u>. —Romans 12:12

Each moment that I stumbled and fell in my recovery process led me to wonder all the more when my full healing would come. All I desired was to be normal! This meant doing the things that regular people did. I wanted to be able to wake up, go to work, come home, maybe even cook, go for a walk in the park; whatever it was that normal people would do daily. I had to keep reminding myself that I was stumbling only because the devil wasn't willing to let go so easily. The moment you choose the path of freedom, the enemy places a target on your back. He wants you bound in darkness and will turn up the heat with several attacks.

But remember that you are a child of God and Romans 12:12 should be your daily antidote: *Rejoicing in hope.* This means that your trust is invested in God, even when the road seems narrow and tough, and that you are always hopeful before and after the victory, resting in the truth that He will always come through. I have put together an acronym for the word H.O.P.E to help reinforce your expressions of it in the face of the onslaught of darkness. **H**aving an **O**ptimistic **P**erspective on **E**verything will determine the outcome of your healing.

You must not allow the enemy to prey on your thoughts, as he will certainly turn them against you. Since your thoughts become your words, start feeding your mind with positive thoughts of freedom and recover. I kept dreaming about the things I was going to do when I received my healing, even though it still seemed distant. I remember always thinking about the many parks I was going to jog and take walks in. As simple as that sounds to a regular person, it never existed for me within the frame of mind of substance abuse. I mean, who wants to go walking or jogging in the park after drinking herself into stupor? No one! I encourage you to get a notebook, give it a nice name and start writing all the things that you are going to do once you recover. That's a practical step to showing forth new HOPE. As surely as God lives, your healing will come! Refuse evil thoughts and, eliminate any thoughts of self-doubt. It doesn't matter how long you have been bound, or what background you come from, or whether the world looks down on you. What matters is that you are a child of God and your life has been preserved till this moment; to experience healing and be a witness to other addicts out there.

    Let these thoughts keep you optimistic. God has already brought you this far, so allow your perspective on life to be transformed through His daily renewal. Let everything in your life breed and speak hope to you!

CHAPTER 7

Be Patient in Tribulation

This is not a scare tactic. Take it as precautionary advice instead. I have mentioned earlier that you will go through trying times as you travel the road to deliverance. Therefore, you need to prepare to endure those difficult times of testing. Trust me, I have been there, and I am certain that God will carry you through. Welcome to Christianity and recovery, you will be tried and tested, but you must stand your ground and remember that healing is in the works. Based on my experience, substance abuse is usually an escape mechanism from hurts, loneliness, depression and other negative feelings and like most addicts, I did not want to confront the reality of those emotions, or of any other thing for that matter.

The greatest challenge, therefore, is that in the wake of recovery, our minds and bodies have no other way of coping with any intense emotion. Hence we get assailed and overwhelmed by a truckload of abruptly unmasked emotions that we are ill prepared to handle. The temptation is to turn right back to alcohol, heroin, cocaine, sex, food, shopping; whatever your poison was, in order to quickly gloss them over. Yet these are the very same things that you need to stay away from, so you need to be especially mindful when the feelings and "nerves" come rushing at you because the devil is also fully prepared to fight you with them till you give in.

Back then, I was clueless about handling my feelings, because when I drank, I couldn't tell what my feelings were or whose feelings might get hurt—I just had no regards for people's feelings and no consideration for my own feelings. I didn't know how to process those feelings rationally without the toxicity of mind altering substances in my body. The enemy was well aware of this weakness, so he tried to use those that were close and dear to me when I started my sober living, to hurt me. This had never been easy to deal with, but to have to handle that with a sober mind? Talk about tribulation! It cut so deep that I would cry for days. I did not understand what was happening. I can't remember the number of times I drove to the liquor store and just sat in the parking lot crying. All my hurts and bruised emotions were tumbling out without restraint.

Holding on to sobriety was extremely difficult for me; the devil was fighting me, and it seems as though the people around me were being nasty. If you are in that situation now, please endure, because that pain is just for a while. You will soon make it out of this. *Rejoice in hope, be patient in tribulation, be constant in prayer. Romans 12:12*

CHAPTER 8

Be Constant in Prayer

This chapter dwells on the latter portion of Romans 12:12, and doubles as the perfect way to end this section. Prayer is the principal tool by which strongholds are destroyed. I remember countless instances where I would cry out in prayer for my healing. Even before coming into Christianity, I still prayed. One thing that I believe proves the existence of God is this; most people believe in praying, regardless of their various religious leanings. The word "pray" is used cross-culturally throughout different religions by both believers and non-believers alike. One of my favorite Church activities is going neighborhood canvassing with the evangelism team; in other words, taking the gospel of Christ to neighborhood residents, and is always an awesome time to witness God's mighty hand at work. I made a most interesting discovery as we knocked on doors to meet all kinds of people.

Many of those we met were not saved, yet when we asked them, "Is there anything you would like our church to pray for?" Prayer request lists surprisingly came tumbling out. Why? Even though they were not in a personal relationship with God, they still acknowledged the efficacy of prayer. They were inadvertently admitting that there is a God, especially considering that they were giving their prayer lists to a bunch of strangers. This profoundly illustrates the power of prayer. There were days that even after I had turned my back and walked away from a house where someone had not accepted more than our evangelism flyer, I still felt fulfilled just knowing I got a prayer request from them.

Prayer is powerful. Therefore you need to pray constantly, not sometimes and certainly not only when you feel like it. It is a spiritual responsibility, one we commit to primarily for our benefit, as it provides a protective shield from the enemy's attacks on your journey to divine healing. So why not stay secure? Prayer is not complicated, so if you do not know how to pray, start off talking to God by acknowledging Him, and thanking Him for your healing. He is your heavenly Father so just pour out your heart to Him. There is no wrong or right way to pray; all that is needed is the outpouring of heartfelt words to God.

Employ the shield of prayer to guard yourself against the enemy's attacks. Right in the midst of my addiction, I prayed. In spite of the fact that I was not feeling righteous at that moment, I still prayed. I asked Him for a healing of which I am a living testimony today. You see, there may be times you find yourself just praying and praying, with no sign of an answer from God. At those times, please understand that God is working things out on your behalf. You may not *feel* it immediately since it's a spiritual process, but your answers are coming in God's timing.

Therefore, always rejoice in hope, be patient in tribulation and continue to pray, for, in the long run, you will witness complete healing unfold in your life. The pursuit of sobriety through Christ is attainable, regardless of your present state. Go ahead and brace yourself for a mighty healing, such as you have never seen before. I am so excited for you because I know, without a doubt, that the Lord will heal! Continue in faith, hope, and persistence, for God is faithful!

CHAPTER 9

The Claws of the Devourer

"As long as you walk this earth, the enemy has a target on your back, and his mission is to destroy God's temple, both the physical body and the church." — Memory Bengesa

The enemy will stop at nothing till he brings down as many people as he can, and his methods remain the same; luring people into sin, eventually resulting in death. He is like a lion and we, his ultimate target prey. Since the days of Adam and Eve, the devil has been roaming the earth, for no other cause than to find a breeding ground in human bodies. Having been in leadership for so many years, I have worked with a lot of people. Some came and went like a revolving door according to their season of life, while some came and eventually got fired, forced to leave due to non-compliance or breach of company policy.

I often observed that employees who had to leave because of school, children, relocation or other personal reasons, would usually have such a peaceful outlook and gracious attitude as they went on to finish off their two-week notice. On the other hand, those who seemed to always have something mischievous up their sleeves, having frustrated management by their attitude, would get the two-week notice and we were almost sure they would finish off amidst dispute and fall-outs if they managed to finish at all.

The disgruntled employee is never fun to deal with because you never know what kind of attitude their bitterness would produce, or what nasty schemes they would attempt to sabotage the company with before their last day of employment. It was always an iffy situation, as they might even attempt to *punish* co-workers through their actions, in order to get back at the company.

However, it was always fascinating to see that in spite of those cheeky attempts, the company as a whole, was never really adversely affected. An incident occurred in which an employee stopped coming to work a few of days after her two-week notice was issued. This person had been in charge of getting the supplies for our department, but instead of bringing back the corporate cards and supplies, she simply decided to hold on to them.

Now the funny part was that one of the other employees had spoken with her, wondering about her sudden absence and the attendant shortage of our supplies. This disgruntled employee stated that she was "mad" at the "higher up's" in the corporate home office all the way in Ohio; a man whose reaction had nothing to do with those in the field! Now, one person's frustrations held others to ransom. The people that suffered the consequences of her actions were the local team, far away from the Ohio office; the people she thought she was actually punishing. The team had to go without those supplies for some days which did not put us out of business, thank goodness, but then, it was an unnecessary inconvenience created by someone's anger against the wrong people.

The LORD said to Satan, "Where have you come from?" Satan answered the LORD, "From roaming through the earth and going back and forth in it." Job 1:7

Now here is the crux of the preceding story. The enemy is not happy with God's past decision to cast him out of heaven. He was one of God's most beautiful creations but had one day gotten arrogant, thinking a little too highly of himself, and God was not going to tolerate such belligerence amongst his angels. The devil suffered the consequences of his actions and has remained bitter and angry at God ever since. Now, who does he take it out on? Us. Human beings! We are caught right in the middle, as the devil is constantly trying to prove a point to God that His precious humans are destructible. The enemy has been at this since the creation of time and figures he can hurt God through us because he knows how much God loves us. He knows that our bodies are the temple of the Lord, and he tries to destroy us by urging us to defile that temple. It took a while, but I finally unraveled the enemy's methods, and it became one of my passports to freedom.

> *"The devil is the master of temporary gratification …and God is the master of permanent satisfaction."*

The enemy keeps us focused only on the present—pleasure, such that we are initially unaware of the growing damage being inflicted on us. All those years, I could feel my body coming apart from my constant alcohol use, but my tormented mind was not thinking, "Oh! Let me watch out for long-term body damage." Focusing on the pleasure at the moment is deadly because a continued pattern of sin eventually leads to death. If I had continued to be bound in such heavy drinking, I would have caused myself some irreparable damage, probably costing me my liver, kidneys and eventually my life.

> *"The enemy is not happy until he kills us from the inside out, through body rot caused by long-term sinful actions!"*
> —*Memory Bengesa*

S.I.N

Satan Is Not Happy (S.I.N)

Why does sin matter within the context of this discussion? It's simple. *Sin is the parent of strongholds.* It always starts off as a thought in the minds of the willing prey, and then it escalates into sin. Ungodly thoughts are sin in themselves, and when we act on them, they lead to more sin, evolving into a snowball effect in no time. Soon the individual becomes bound to their sin, and thus, a stronghold is created. As I reflect on the early days of my addiction before it actually became one, all it started with was a seeming defiant gulp of one bottle of beer, and how strangely good it had made me feel at the time. After that, my tongue simply craved the taste of the substance that made me feel temporarily ecstatic, and then one bottle wasn't enough any longer.

So, I had two, and when they were not enough, I had three... on and on until it became a monstrous addiction eating me up. But I never thought it would get that bad. On the night that Tony offered me that first bottle of beer, I could have remained adamant. Instead, some part of me thought, "What's the big deal anyway?" That same part of me did not consider the long-term consequences as I drank that twelve-ounce bottle. This often reminds me of Eve. I think that deep within her, she didn't take that bite of the forbidden fruit in hopes of getting kicked out of Eden. She probably did so out of sheer curiosity, maybe just to test the claims the enemy had planted in her mind. At that moment, she probably was not considering the possibility of any long-term consequences.

I'd like to share what I consider to be the pattern of sin, so you are better equipped to avoid it. I coined an acronym for S.I.N which translates to **Satan Is N**ot happy! He is not happy about your attempts to get well and is certainly very displeased with your decision to walk closer to God. As a matter of fact, he is not happy about humans at all, especially believers in Christ; how could God have created anyone in His own image and likeness just to spite him?!

> *Be sober-minded; be watchful. Your adversary, the devil, prowls around like a roaring lion, seeking someone to devour.*
> *– 1 Peter 5:8*

Dear friends, I write this book with great compassion in my heart, being a former prisoner to the hold of darkness. Understand that all things begin in the mind; good or evil, victory or defeat. Therefore, it is our Christian duty to sync our minds with God's will. Addiction does not just happen. It is a process that grows over time because we feed it with the numerous lies the enemy has told us. In this next section, I would be highlighting some key words to keep in mind as you defend yourself in this warfare!

> *"Sin practiced over an extended period of time without repentance, often leads to the bondage of strongholds."*
> —*Memory Bengesa*

Do not be L.E.D into sin by the enemy; **L**ured, **E**nticed and **D**esire (James 1:14-15). Consider the fall of man at Eden. The very same schemes devised by the devil in that Garden, remain useful to him to this day. The enemy may not always be predictable, but his conniving ways and deceitful schemes are repetitive. The great thing is that we have the Bible to help us understand the various methods of the enemy such that we are not left ignorant of his devices. So, as opposed to an unfair fight in which we do not know who our opponent is, or how he operates, this, dear friends, is an incredibly fair fight! There are three crucial aspects to the temptation that, when combined, would surely lead to a fall.

I sincerely hope that you properly grasp these aspects, especially as they relate individually to you, so you can stand fast and be watchful, wielding the right weaponry for the battle. In an earlier chapter, we discussed the harmful pattern of making excuses to justify our sin. However, in this section, I would be sharing on how it all begins with the attack of the enemy's lies on the mind, which in turn, leads to a sinful act, and then repeatedly fueled by the lies of self-justification such that it creates and sustains a sinful pattern which ultimately becomes a full-blown stronghold. Here is how the process works:

> *"A lie from the enemy in a thought process + self-justification = deeper and perpetual sin. Perpetual sin without repentance leads to bondage, and bondage over time becomes a stronghold."—Memory Bengesa*

CHAPTER 10

Lured

But the serpent said (the start of the conversation in which the enemy is planting his seed of lie in her mind) to the woman, "You will not surely die. For God knows that when you eat of it your eyes will be opened, and you will be like God, knowing good and evil. – Genesis 3:4-5

I remember that in my struggle to recover, the enemy's favorite lie to me was "rationing." I felt that I had no problem because I limited myself to a certain amount of alcohol. The enemy had me believing that alcoholics could not stop drinking once they started, so for the longest time, I felt as though I was normal because I religiously restricted myself to the same number of alcoholic beverages each night. The biggest lie that was out to kill me lay in my justification. In reality, it was not how many alcoholic beverages I had, but how much alcohol each beverage actually contained, which upon reflection now, was way more than I should ever have consumed at any given time!

Had I continued to pride in the number of beverages I could stick to and had the Lord not saved me, that justification would by now have placed me in line for a liver or kidney transplant, maybe even death from alcohol poisoning! And in any case, the enemy was out to kill me. The point is that the enemy will lure us with a small lie; small enough to trigger a "little" justification, and if you buy into it, you will get hooked. Please understand that the end of all sin is death. I rode on my self-justification, and it kept me enslaved to alcohol for years. I thought I was normal, *"What...so what, I like to drink every night! I only take a couple of drinks before bed anyways."* And for nine years, I was bound to that lie!

Eve experienced the selfsame thing. *"But the serpent said to the woman, you will not surely die. For God knows that when you eat of it, your eyes will be opened, and you will be like God, knowing good and evil. Genesis 3:4-5.* The only difference between you and Eve is that today, we are most unlikely to be approached by a hissing snake asking us to sin; the enemy's lies are aimed at our minds instead. A slinking snake trying to have a conversation is a tad too obvious, even for the devil! What may seldom be obvious, however, are the subtle suggestions of the enemy in the mind, often disguised as harmless thoughts.

You've got to be mindful of the thoughts that manifest themselves in your life. Never ever succumb to any justification for sinful thoughts. A sex addict's justification might go something like this, *"I will just sleep with this **one** person; I don't suppose I have a problem since I'm getting all the pleasure I need from a single sex partner."* That one partner might have an incurable ailment, now what? One person would have gotten you entangled in their mess, and the enemy will begin to feel victorious over your life. For that person struggling with drug abuse with needle use, their justification sounds somewhat like, *"I do not share my needles with anyone, so I'm sure I do not have a problem."* But what if you hit the wrong artery and or vein while injecting?

That could well be the end of your life! For the food addict, their justification may go like this: *"I am not addicted, I just love good food, and it makes me happy."* That next bite could lead to high cholesterol levels and eventually heart disease. And if there is no disease already, a poor eating lifestyle can also place them in a deathbed sooner than desired. Refuse to be lured by the enemy by keeping him out of your thought process, and if you ever get confused deciphering your thoughts from the devil's suggestions, always remember that Satan means no good.

So, for every thought that is followed by justification, I suggest you pray, because God's thoughts towards you are good and perfect, never confusing and requiring no excuses to justify them.

"Satan is thrilled when he rules over your body. Your body is the temple of God, and Satan desperately seeks to tear it down, whether it is your body or the physical church; he wants to make a mockery out of you."—Memory Bengesa

CHAPTER II

Enticed

Now the serpent was more <u>crafty</u> (he will be very discreet, and he has the time and patience to work on you) than any other beast of the field that the LORD God had made. He said to the woman, "<u>Did God actually say</u>, '<u>You shall not eat of any tree in the garden'?</u>" —Genesis 3:1

The enemy is very manipulative. In the above verse, he entices Eve with a question so that she can think about it, mull over it and begin to doubt its truth. Truth be told, that is what I call the *question of condemnation.* The enemy places questions in our minds, hoping to prey upon our tendency to overthink things. He always enticed me with one appealing question or another, with an aim to get me to think up an unreasonable answer that satisfied my need to go ahead with the sin. Sadly, it seemed to work against me for a very long time. For instance, Sister A is driving home after a church meeting and is recapping the evening's events when suddenly she thinks of the new lady who joined their meeting, sister B. Sister B was in the meeting venue, handling the minutes for the meeting and though she is not new to the church, she was new to that meeting. Sister A is now thinking of the short conversation she had with sister B after the meeting, *"Wait, was she speaking a little loudly when we talked?"* (The question of condemnation is manifesting in sister A's mind).

It could then develop into: "*I don't know who she thinks she was raising her voice at like that?!*" (Sister A is getting all worked up now, and the enemy is getting excited because he is beginning to get a foot in the door of her heart). Then it escalates into: "*I knew she did not like me from the way she was looking at me while I was speaking.*" and then it spirals further into, "*Well...I do not like her either! She should not have raised her voice at me, how disrespectful!*" This then snowballs into an individual walking around mad at another person whom she 'thinks' does not care for her because of the presumed tone of voice used in a previous conversation. Now, in this analogy, the person who unconsciously raised her voice had meant no harm; that is just her speech style.

Consider how the whole issue started off with a question of condemnation entertained by sister A and in no time, the enemy had her convinced that sister B disliked her. The enemy snuck in and simply amplified her other weaknesses such as insecurity, jealousy, and resentment. Now the enemy has set up shop in sister A's mind, such that every time sister B walks by in the hallway, she is met with feelings of hate and anger. And over what?!

"A question of condemnation is the tool the enemy uses to crack your door open and make you unwittingly receptive to his devices."—Memory Bengesa

I remember one particular event; I had remained substantially sober. I had thought that after those four weeks I was doing really well. I suppose I wanted so bad to convince myself that I was not an addict, so I attempted to *push* myself to sobriety. I should have known that without God, I was an open target to the enemy. During my rehab course, as I have shared earlier, a friend got some free baseball tickets, with great seats. Before leaving for the event, I left my card and cash at home because I didn't want to buy any alcohol at the stadium. I wanted to enjoy the game in my sober mind. While we were at our seats, forty-five minutes into the game, my friend's father came by. Because I was focused on the game, I did not see him arrive, all I felt was a tap on the shoulder from my friend as she was trying to get my attention.

I leaned towards her, my eyes still on the game, and then she mentioned, "*Dad is here and wants to know which beer you want?*" Wait, what? My neck swiveled to the left then, to see her dad standing there and sure enough, he was selling beer and peanuts at the stadium! Really! So, initially I thought I could resist this temptation because I believed that drinks sold anywhere around a stadium were expensive, but then I thought, "Here is a free one!" Well, there was not much thinking after that and I took that cup without so much as a consideration of my four-week milestone. That four-week milestone disappeared as fast as the suds disappeared from my cup. Here is where the question of condemnation became enticing; all I thought when I saw her father was, "free alcohol!" (The initial enticement by the enemy came up in my mind). I made a feeble attempt to explain that I deliberately left my wallet at home, but my friend said, "It's on the house."

When I heard that, I thought, *Time to drink up!* As the rounds kept coming, I kept thinking, "it is free!" This was the lie that led to condemnation, and a relapse that was terminal! All from a question. Another consistent lie with which the enemy kept me bound to my addiction, was the fear of the unknown. Every time I tried to quit, the enemy had me wondering whether I would be miserable if I never got to have a drink ever again. While I was in my recovery program, I kept worrying that I would never have a drink again. I would consider it, and my thoughts would quickly spiral into despair. I remember one time sitting and thinking, "Okay! I can do this recovery program, but I do not know if I can never have a drink, ever again in my life." I would dwell on what I could not drink at weddings, parties, new-years celebrations, Cinco de Mayo, my birthday "turn-up," Jesus Birthday, St Pattys day, 4th of July—the list of justifiable drinking events was endless!

The question of condemnation the devil had me preoccupied with was this; "I can never drink—ever again in life?" And then the response would quickly follow; *"Who said you cannot drink ever again? Once you get out of recovery, you can try drinking in moderation."* Well, guess what? That was not working; I was an addict, and that meant there was no moderation in my world!

CHAPTER 12

Desire

> *But each person is <u>tempted</u> when he is <u>lured</u> and <u>enticed</u> by his <u>own desire</u>. Then <u>desire</u> when it has conceived gives <u>birth to sin</u>, and sin when it is fully grown brings forth death.*
> —James 1:14-15

I would like to emphasize the importance of one's desire towards anything. Other than the three main steps to my complete healing which I would be sharing further on in this read, one pertinent concept I had to struggle to master was desire. In spite of how much I seemed to be "trying" to get myself to give up my addiction after rehab, quitting remained just a mirage; I simply lacked the desire to quit. The thought of quitting was often driven by my association with my church regimen, meaning, because I was feeling convicted as I went to church while still battling an addiction, I felt like a hypocrite. Because of that, I "tried" my best to quit but all to no avail. Desire is a double-edged sword.

When used for evil, it can bring one into sin, and when used for good, it is also able to lead to healing. My attitude during outpatient rehab as well as the journey afterward was only a reflection of my lack of desire to be truly healed. I simply had no will to commit to the meetings. There is absolutely nothing wrong with rehab and meetings. Even though I failed after completing the program, I learned a lot of useful things while in rehab. So, I am certainly not encouraging you to quit any program or meeting that may aid your recovery; please stay committed to whatever works for you. I fell off the wagon of sobriety due to my lack of desire to stick with the program, and as a result, I relapsed and remained confined to my addiction. Had I continued in ignorance, there is no telling where I would have been… or been buried today.

I can testify that when I started attending church, my desire to be closer to God helped me tremendously in my recovery process. The more I went to church, the more I desired God, and the more I desired God, the more I desired to please Him. And with every day that His desire grew within me, my desire for substance gradually faded till I eventually broke free.

By the time God delivered me, it had been a total of nine years that I had been bound to my addiction. As I remained hopeful on the road to recovery, I used to imagine that my healing would come with a fancy supernatural big bang, or that I would encounter an angel in a dream and suddenly wake up healed. I really dwelt on several picturesque thoughts of what healing would feel like, as all I could do was "fantasize" as I awaited complete deliverance. Who would have thought that the day would be anything but dramatic? I would like to crave your indulgence to allow me to continue the description of this particular experience in the last section titled "FREE." And for a good reason too.

DELIVERED

Right before my final healing, the Lord placed on my heart the importance of the cord of Faith, Believing and Knowing. I briefly shared on faith in earlier sections, and now I would like to discuss this three-fold cord that every addict or struggling Christian needs to grasp to begin their healing process. Understand that believing is having the faith that knows without a doubt, that God will heal you.

CHAPTER 13

Faith

And as Jesus passed on from there, two <u>blind</u> men followed him, <u>crying aloud</u>, "<u>Have mercy on us</u>, Son of David." ²⁸ When he entered the house, the <u>blind men came to him</u>, and Jesus said to them, "<u>Do you believe that I am able to do this?</u>" They said to him, "<u>Yes, Lord.</u>" ²⁹ Then he touched their eyes, saying, "<u>According to your faith</u> be it done to you." ³⁰ And their eyes were opened. And Jesus sternly warned them, "See that no one knows about it." ³¹ But they went away and spread his fame through all that district. —Matthew 9:27-31

This scripture is deeply profound; there were two men who without their sight, could yet feel the presence of Christ enough to instantly know, that He could help them out. Lost in my addiction and blind to all spiritual truth, I still somehow knew that if I prayed and held on long enough, God was going to heal me. It might seem as though you are right now in the most challenging time of your life, and it feels like God is nowhere in the vicinity. You have prayed, fasted and given your all to the Lord and yet you are still stuck in the "struggle" with an addiction; be encouraged, dear one.

Continue seeking the Lord. If two blind men could feel Christ's presence and the nudge of repentance as they cried out to him, then you can also be healed. So many people misunderstand the concept of faith, assuming that mentally or verbally expressing that you have it is all there is to it. Faith is tangible, found within us as an action. People can profess day and night that "they have faith," as if it's in their back pocket, just waiting to be pulled out and placed on a mantle when terrible storms hit. But by the time the tides wear off, they begin to search for the faith they used to have as though it has been misplaced. Your faith in God needs to be more of an action that is manifested from within you.

The blind men did not sit around where they lived and "have faith" that Christ would heal them, rather they moved (action) in the direction of Christ. They actually cried out as they followed Him, determined to get their healing. Abraham is described as the father of "Faith" because he always moved towards whatever God commanded him to do. If you have been verbally exercising your faith, today is the day that you set your faith in motion and walk towards Christ, crying out in repentance.

When an altar call is made, be sure to respond by stepping out (action) in faith. When there is a revival in town or at your local church, endeavor to move (action) in faith for healing. Always be in motion for God, looking for and following Him via all avenues available to you. I love my home church, but at the same time, I was often found at tent revivals, all night prayer meetings, and on mobile prayer lines. I knew that my deliverance from addiction required more than just sitting on my basement stairs every night saying a prayer; I had to keep following Christ and crying out for my healing, seeking Him where and when He could be found. The blind men gravitated towards Jesus, even though they could not see Him. They knew they needed to move close enough to receive their healing.

I encourage you to keep on moving towards Christ for your healing, even when you feel alone or feel that God is nowhere near. Continue moving towards Him.

CHAPTER 14

Believe

And behold, a woman who had suffered from a discharge of blood for twelve years came up behind him and touched the <u>fringe</u> of his garment, for she <u>said to herself,</u> "If I only touch his garment, I will be made well." Jesus turned, and seeing her he said, "Take heart, daughter; your <u>faith has made you well.</u>" And instantly the woman was made well.

I marvel all the time when I read the above passage of the "bleeding woman." This was a woman with an embarrassing problem. My best guess is, not a lot of people knew about her problem and my second-best guess is that she most likely kept it carefully hidden due to its nature. Men may be unable to fully relate to this but consider it from this perspective; her embarrassing ailment is somewhat analogous to addiction. No one readily admits to addiction, and the few who do usually ensure that it is hidden away from family and friends, just like I did. I intentionally never mentioned my drinking problem to anyone, as I was embarrassed by it and scared of what they would think or say about me.

After all, addicts were often laughed at and stigmatized, so I decided that I'd rather not become the punch line to anyone's cruel jokes. In addition, I thought that anyone I told would begin to feel sorry for me or become overbearing when I was out with them. I shared the above to point out, that anyone can relate to the shame of that bleeding woman. Even in the darkest days of my addiction,

I never stopped believing that God was going to heal me, and I went on to denounce the label "alcoholic."

I kept telling myself that someday it was going to be over and I would finally be free. I engaged the power of positive affirmations, and I sincerely encourage you to apply it, as it aided my process greatly. Write those words on your bathroom mirror if you have to. Write in whatever language you prefer, in whatever medium available, on whichever surface closest to you; just do whatever it takes to get positive words and thoughts into your mind till they truly become your truth. The woman with the bleeding issue knew that she had to speak out her beliefs so that her own ears could hear them, and her mind would believe them.

Whatever you believe for, must first come alive within so that you begin to manifest it in day-to-day living. Once the hemorrhaging woman declared her belief out loud, she then proceeded to touch the fringe of Jesus's garment! She was certain that she did not need to touch His arm, His feet, or the cloth itself; all she needed to be made whole, was that itty-bitty portion of Christ's garment. Some people want to be delivered, but because they have been bound for so long, they have lost the ability to believe that it will ever happen. Do not listen to that lie of the devil for even one more second! The hemorrhaging woman had been bleeding for twelve years; twelve years of physical and emotional pain, twelve years of extreme weakness and misery, yet colored with glimpses of hope. Twelve years is a long time, but she simply would not give up on herself. Tell me, how long have you been bound? Twenty years? Forty years? A hundred? God can and will set you free and trust me when I say that you are better off being delivered by God alone because then, you are assured that you are heaven-bound. Alcohol was all I had known for nine years of my life. Those years were full of struggles, a series of alcohol counseling sessions and failed attempts at quitting.

I occasionally became skeptical about God's ability to help me and would sometimes wonder why He would not bail me out each time I took steps to quit until He finally made me understand that I had to stop "trying" so hard and instead start "believing" in

Him to deliver me. Let your belief in God's deliverance "Be-Alive" (believe) in you for your complete healing to come through.

CHAPTER 15

Know

"To believe is to make faith alive in you, to have faith is to move in action according to what you believe, and belief is to <u>know</u> that it is done in you through Christ." — Memory Bengesa

The ability to know that your deliverance is underway takes a certain degree of strength, but when you believe and have faith, then knowing is secondary. Your addiction will only last for a season, and if you believe this, then you will be delivered. But if you accept it as a lifelong sentence, then you will have difficulty overcoming it. I call it a season because like every other difficult situation in your life, it will eventually pass. Remember that like the blind men, you have to find Jesus, follow Him, pray and actually have faith that He will heal you. Like the woman with the "bleeding issue," it's never how long you've been addicted, it is about your adamant pursuit of Christ and willingness to get close to Him. The freedom that comes with being healed should always be the goal.

FREE

The Spirit of the Lord is upon me because he has anointed me to proclaim good news to the poor. He has sent me to proclaim liberty to the captives and recovering of sight to the blind, to set at liberty those who are oppressed. – Luke 4:18

Our sins were paid for over 2000 years ago, and I am excited to let you know that God cleanses all sin, no matter how terrible. What matters is that you do realize right now that the enemy is taking advantage of you through this addiction and leading you out of God's best for your life. Be assured that God has great plans for you. While I believed and knew, right in the midst of my addiction, that my healing would come, I certainly had no idea what God had planned out for me after recovery, neither could I have believed them possible. If anyone had told me that I was going to be an author, I would have rolled my eyes and maybe laughed it off. But that is how beautifully God works; He brings you out of the lies of the enemy and makes the very best out of your life. The devil initially had me imprisoned in the lie that I was an alcoholic, and it was all I would ever be. I never really thought I would rise up to be an influential voice for the Lord.

Every time I consider all that God has done for me, I simply stand in awe. He took a supposed alcoholic and outcast and created a new person in her; he polished me and raised me up for His glory! Never doubt that God has special plans for you, and He cannot fulfill those plans when your body is a breeding ground for the enemy. God wants to use you in ways that you have never imagined, for His glory. You might not feel so special while struggling through an addiction, but I assure you, that you will ALWAYS be special in God's eyes. He is our Creator and our Redeemer. I want you to know that God is waiting specifically for you, and ready to use you. He loves you so much that He does not care about your past anymore, but rather He is concerned about your present and the glorious future ahead.

For God so loved the world, that he gave his only Son, that whoever believes in him should not perish but have eternal life.
–John 3:16

CHAPTER 16

The Principal Ingredient

When one is cooking and following a recipe, it would be impossible to achieve that intended scrumptious dish without the "main" ingredient. Simply put, it won't be chocolate without cocoa, and it certainly won't be bread without the flour; neither would it ever taste the same without their most important ingredients. The principal ingredient for healing and deliverance is salvation. I have earnestly sought the Lord, and I sincerely trust the Holy Spirit to help present this subject of salvation to you in the most effective and individually relevant manner.

I would love to tell you that simply reading my book will give you all the answers you need to be healed of your addiction, but it goes beyond just getting healed. I must share this with you as I have a responsibility under God to help you understand that you can only begin to truly appreciate your state of *disease* and seek the Lord in a deeper sense for healing, by understanding salvation. Salvation does not seek to give you instant physical healing without doing a thorough job in you from within. Salvation causes your eyes to be opened to the truth, helping you to become more aware of every deception of the enemy. With salvation comes an everlasting life through God. I cannot force salvation on you as it has to be a personal decision taken with understanding.

But I greatly urge you, even if you aren't sure that you need it, to seek the lord about it and allow Him to help and lead you through that decision. Everything that will be discussed in the following chapters are hinged solely on the subject of salvation. Therefore I hope that your heart will be open as I go on to share my salvation experience with you. It was not until the day I genuinely accepted Christ with a remorseful heart that my healing process truly began. At that moment, I instantly received an opening of the eyes; all the tactics and wiles of the enemy began to unfold right before me and as they did, the stronger my resolve became to remain in Christ and the more certain I was that God was going to heal me. Without a doubt, the main ingredient for breaking any stronghold and receiving healing is through the understanding of salvation. This is a truth you must accept, to begin with; every other concept you think you have learned holds no value without this foundation. Without receiving salvation, you will remain in the dark and continue to be a working vessel for the enemy's use, deceived and bound by him. If some stranger came up to you and offered you the keys to your dream house, fully paid for and tastefully furnished, and all this stranger asked in return was to be allowed to live in the cottage on the property, how would you respond? This is all God wants. He has the keys to your eternal life of happiness, and all he wants is that you allow him to live in your heart, and everything else is already paid for.

    Your sins were paid for at the cross where Jesus died; yours is to accept an eternal life through God. Dear one, please allow God to open your eyes as He did mine and let him break the stronghold of addiction in your life completely. I love you so much, and my greatest desire is to enjoy this freely-given life with you in pure joy, free from all darkness. And it is possible; total healing is just at your fingertips. Of every decision I have ever made, choosing to surrender my life to God will always be my best! For nothing in the world can ever compare to God's greatness and goodness.

CHAPTER 17

Redemption

Jesus said to him, "I am the way, and the truth, and the life. No one comes to the Father except through me.
— John 14-16

    I gave my life to the Lord a few months after I returned to church, and it was by far, the most awesome feeling I ever had. The feeling I got when I first confessed Christ at the age of 12 could not be compared to it. At that tender age, I had honestly thought I surrendered my life to Christ wholeheartedly, but I realized later that I did it only because everyone was doing it. When I accepted Jesus this second time, however, I was fired up as I left the altar, wanting to change everything about me the best I knew how.

    I wanted to tell everyone about Jesus, my new-found Love until the *honeymoon* was over, and I began to struggle with trying to be a "new creature." My addiction was tugging at me by the throat, and I fell smack-dab into full drinking mode. "What have I done?" I thought sorrowfully, overwhelmed with guilt as the weight of my actions bore down on me. I tried in the early stages of my conversion, to skip church, feeling as though I had tainted myself and fallen "backward" but unbeknownst to me, I was still a new creature. God was not done with me, and the saints at my church would not let me skip church anymore, so I continued going to our services and meetings, though struggling with my addiction. I knew that I had to stay within the covering of God. Sure, there were nights that I cried because my heart longed to do what was right, but my body wanted to do otherwise, and there were times that I disappointed the church by not showing up to help out at some events because my flesh had chosen to binge-drink.

I felt like a hypocrite, but I never stopped going to church. Like the woman with the bleeding issue, I knew that my time of deliverance would come. While I was out in the world, I had been so naïve as to think that my healing would come the minute I accepted Christ as my personal Lord and Savior but that was not the case. Please understand that I do not judge you and I have no reason to lie just to tell anyone what they want to hear. I am here to help you as the Lord guides me. Having been in Christ, and in church for some time now, I can tell you that we've all got issues. Some people's issues are worrisome, while some others have theirs in check. Whatever your situation is, I encourage you to remain in church until God delivers you, and even after that. You must understand that you need spiritual covering from the guilt and condemnation the enemy may send your way. The guilt I carried was enough to keep me out of the church, but when I overcame it, God was able to continue working in me. The world often regards Christians as picture perfect people, yet the truth simply is that we are not angels floating around without flaws.

You may walk into church one sunny Sunday morning and find your pastor teaching specifically on your addiction and speaking strongly against such habits, causing you to feel somewhat attacked. This is a good time to exercise patience and understand that they are probably unaware of your struggles and are only teaching what God has laid upon their heart. Accept that sermon as God's healing word and take it as another opportunity to talk to the Lord about those struggles. And keep going to church! Even if you overhear some members saying negative things about addicts, don't take it personally that they are being judgmental and devoid of love and acceptance towards others. Don't let the devil drive you away from God's presence. He doesn't want you there.

The process of redemption helped me to understand my place in God's kingdom, and my church regimen was the perfect path for that divine integration. I was fed with the word each time I was in service and remaining in fellowship with the saints helped me to stay grounded while preventing me from feeling alone. The first step to your spiritual recovery is redemption.

So if the Son sets you free, you will be free indeed.
– John 8:36

Because if you confess with your mouth that Jesus is Lord and if you believe in your heart that God raised him from the dead, you will be saved. For with the heart one believes and is justified, and with the mouth, one confesses and is saved. For the Scripture says, "Everyone who believes in him will not be put to shame." For there is no distinction between Jew and Greek, for the same Lord is Lord of all, bestowing his riches on all who call on him. For everyone who calls on the name of the Lord will be saved.
– Romans 10:9-13

For the wages of sin is death, but the free gift of God is eternal life in Christ Jesus our Lord.
–Romans 6:23

Therefore, if anyone is in Christ, he is a new creation. The old has passed away; behold, the new has come.
–2 Corinthians 5:17

Let it be known to you, therefore, brothers, that through this man forgiveness of sins is proclaimed to you, and by him, everyone who believes is freed from everything from which you could not be freed by the Law of Moses.
– Acts 13:38-39

For God so loved the world, that he gave his only Son, that whoever believes in him should not perish but have eternal life. For God did not send his Son into the world to condemn the world, but in order that the world might be saved through him.
– John 3:16-17

Prayer for Salvation

If you are ready right now to surrender your life to God, and you believe in your heart that Jesus is Lord and He died for you and will confess with your mouth, you will be saved. Pray these words, and when you are done, please be accountable by becoming a member of the body of Christ. Find a church in which you can be planted if you have not done so yet.

Dear Heavenly Father, I come to you today confessing and admitting my sins before you. I believe in my heart that you sent your Son to die for my sins and that He rose again. I repent of all my sins and turn my life around today to follow you and to remain under your supervision for the rest of my life. I renounce hell today and accept the promised eternal life; in the name of Jesus, thy will be done. Amen. I love you so much, and I want you to get ready for healing. Brace yourself for a total life change! As you enter into the battlefield to fight for what belongs to God, rest assured that, in the name of Jesus and by the blood of Jesus, strongholds will be loosed! Call upon the name of Jesus, plead the blood of Jesus, and lean on the Holy Spirit.

CHAPTER 18

Reconciliation

All this is from God, who through Christ reconciled us to himself and gave us the ministry of reconciliation;
—2 Corinthians 5:18

Reconciliation is the second part of my three-step total recovery through Christ. Throughout this book, I have expressed more than once that as shameful and sad as it was, I was still struggling with my addiction even after I had returned to church. It was not until God delivered me that He showed me His three-step total recovery agenda. After I was redeemed, God had to start working in me from the inside out, purging all that had been built up in me over the nine years of addiction, in addition to the earlier stages of my life. I like to describe reconciliation as God's attempt at bringing you unto Himself, from salvation to justification, and then sanctification. That's why you need that prayer of salvation, as a starting point. It stands as your faith response to God's attempt at reconciling you to Himself through Jesus Christ.

God is indeed awesome! He knew exactly why I kept failing to quit all along. I was not binge drinking for show or leisure; it had become an addiction camouflaging as truth to me. I was broken, hurt, abused, bitter, suffering from a low self-esteem, and alcohol was serving as a relief from those feelings I had about myself. Based on God's revelation, I now realize that the reason I was having numerous relapses, was that I was not healed on the inside. Rehab had only offered me superficial healing. Every attempt I made to quit for those short periods was only aimed at healing on the outside. I just wanted to feel normal, yet it ran deeper than that; my need for healing was not about feeling or looking normal but was really about being normal in God. The reason I could continue in my addiction even when I was in church and had surrendered my life to God was that God was still in the process of purging the inner me. I had to be <u>delivered</u>. And that is why you cannot quit going to church, believing that feeding yourself the Word at home will work perfectly.

God created you for fellowship; you're a part of the Body of Christ, and you need others to minister nourishment to you. As I kept pressing my way into the house of the Lord despite the empty beer bottles at home, God began peeling my inner layers like an onion, one layer at a time. And the more He kept peeling, the more I was gaining strength in Him through faith. All of a sudden, my confidence was rising, I started to dress and feel a little better even though my addiction still lingered. I kept going to church and basking in God's word, and the next thing I realized was that all my anger, disappointment, bitterness, hurt and hate had seeped out over time. I really was feeling better from the inside out.

I smiled more, and I started to drink less. Soon, the purging and healing progressed deep into the recesses of my mind. He set out some small tests that made me gravitate towards Him and helped strengthen my faith. The more He gave me the tests, the more I started to desire and draw closer to Him, but my addiction yet lingered. I was moving into sanctification; God's purifying program, through the power of His Word and Spirit. So, when you find yourself battling mistakes right in the midst of your growing relationship with God, don't give up thinking Christianity isn't working for you. Never believe that lie!

CHAPTER 19

Restored

I will restore to you the years that the swarming locust has eaten, the hopper, the destroyer, and the cutter, my great army, which I sent among you. You shall eat in plenty and be satisfied, and praise the name of the LORD your God, who has dealt wondrously with you. And my people shall never again be put to shame. — Joel 2:25-26

As I earlier explained, my addiction was still present, yet God continued to do a great work in me. I never stopped going to church, and God taught me to draw close to Him in times of trials and tribulations, no matter what came my way. As imperfect as I was in my addiction, I still clung onto God and always hoped for the best from Him. While I had somehow thought my healing would happen as dramatically as the "season finale" to a daytime TV show, and you can't fault me for thinking that way, I never ended up seeing any bright light on my way to the liquor store, nor did any angels visit me in my sleep. It was a Saturday afternoon in August, and I had my stash of alcohol in the refrigerator.

Each time I attempted to quit, I would decide to drink double, if not triple the amount of alcohol I usually had, as a sort of good-bye ritual to my drinking. But a day later, I would find myself back at it again. I would feel completely disgusted with myself that I overdrank on my "supposed" goodbye party of one! Well, this particular Saturday afternoon, I was lounging at home, and I was free from household chores, then I headed to the refrigerator like I always did. After opening it, I stared at it for about five minutes. I bent down and reached for the case of alcohol, placed it on my counter, opened them, one bottle at a time and emptied them in the sink. I grabbed the empty bottles and did not even bother to throw them in my kitchen trash can. I went into the garage and threw them in the main trash can. I got in my car and went for some ice cream and then returned home.

    I watched television until I fell asleep on the couch. The next day, I went to church like I normally did, had a great service, went back home and got ready for the week. I knew in my heart that I was healed but I had not quite past one day yet, so I only rejoiced quietly. By Wednesday evening, I had not made a stop at the liquor store, I knew for sure I was done with my addiction. It was now Friday, and I was at home watching TV with no cravings, tremors, or any thoughts of drinking. It was official; I had finally been delivered. When days turned into months and months turned into years, I knew that the blood of Jesus had healed me.

    Today, I look back on all my failed attempts, and I am convinced that the blood of Jesus set me free. God took away my desire for my addiction and placed in me a deeper desire for Him; that is the best exchange anyone could ever have. I live my life today in full happiness, contentment, love, and peace because God delivered me from the bondage of addiction. I cannot say this enough; God will take away your desires for your addiction for good if you allow Him to. In all my months of sobriety through Christ, I have never had a relapse, and I truly believe it's because I no longer have the desire. Before I came to Christ, I knew there were certain places and events I absolutely had to avoid because they could trigger my drinking. Today, all of that is gone.

    I go wherever I need to and still have zero-desire for the bottles. I only have a desire for Christ. God's restoring power takes away evil desires and replaces them with godly ones. I once craved alcohol, but now, all I desire is Christ and everything He represents to me and humanity. I desire to live for Him alone, I enjoy writing books that can inspire people, I love helping addicts and just to list a few. A year after my healing, I was in my old neighborhood and stopped at the convenience store where I used to purchase my alcohol. The clerks were still there, and one of them wondered, "We have not seen you in a while. Where have you been?" I boldly told them I had found Jesus. They roared in laughter, clearly thinking I was joking until they noticed that I was purchasing a can of soda. One of them was already picking out my usual choice of liquor, but I glanced over, shook my head and said, "No. Thanks." The other clerk was shocked, "What! No alcohol?" I simply replied "Nope! I found Jesus." And guess what, I never went back to that convenience store since that incident because *I do not need to stand trial or endure temptation.*

    I AM RESTORED INDEED! I am glad that I stayed grounded in God, His word, and His church. Please understand that I am still human; I may have crossed that hurdle in my life that was characterized by struggles with sin and fleshly desires, but once in a while, life still throws me its fair share of trials and tribulations which are not addiction related. However, my joy today arises from knowing that if I could overcome the greatest trial of my life, then I can take on anyone or anything that comes my way. With faith and a wonderful knowledge of God, I am more than a conqueror through Christ Jesus.

About the Author

Memory Bengesa is a Zimbabwean Millennial Author, Speaker and CEO that spends most of her time writing in America, her book genres are a conglomerate of both inspirational/motivational non-fiction books to Contemporary Fiction Novels and Screenplays, Memory has contributed some small published articles to various organizations; all of Memory's writings are inspired by her faith. Visit her website for a full bio

www.MemoryBengesa.com

www.MemoryBengesa.com
www.facebook.com/bookmemorybengesa/
MemoryBengesa@Instagram
MemoryBengesa@Twitter
MemoryBengesa@YouTube
#OVERCOME&BEFREE

PERSONAL COMMITMENT PLAN

First Name	Last Name	Date

Conviction Goals

List what your convictions are in each category to continually remind yourself

I have Faith that:	I Believe that:	I Know:

Put on the whole armor of God, that you may be able to stand against the schemes of the devil. –Ephesians 6:11

Renewal Goals

List the things God has to purge out of you to get you to ultimate healing.

Redemption	Reconciliation	Restoration
I am a believer because:	God purge my:	I Desire:

****It is advisable that you discuss your addiction problems in strict confidence with a trusted person, who can help and support you through the process of recovery; preferably a brother* or sister in the faith, or better still, the pastor at your local church. However, please be very discerning when choosing whom to trust and be accountable to.

> *Put on the whole armor of God that you may be able to stand against the schemes of the devil. –Ephesians 6:11*

National helpline 800-662-HELP(4357)

Disclaimer: This book is not a substitution for your current program, rehab and or any medications; this book is for leisure reading and knowledge stimulation.

Published Books:
Purchase your copy and or get more info at:
www.MemoryBengesa.com

- The Sameness Life of Nandi *Novel*
- The Millennial and The Work Place *How to get ahead in your career and stay ahead*
- Born Again Afresh *How Struggling Christians can get back on track*
- FREE *Overcoming Addiction through the power of God*

www.ingramcontent.com/pod-product-compliance
Lightning Source LLC
Chambersburg PA
CBHW032024040426
42448CB00006B/714